Japanese Temari for Beginners

Chapter One
    Introduction to Temari

Chapter Two
    Equipment

Chapter Three
    Secure the thread tail

Chapter Four
    Prepare the Paper Strip for Division Marking (orange Segments).

Chapter Five
    Creating Divisions

Chapter Six
    Mark Stitching Points with Pins

Chapter Seven
    completed Temari

Chapter One

Introduction to Temari

Temari, an exquisite form of traditional Japanese handcraft, has captivated hearts with its intricate beauty and delicate artistry for centuries. Derived from the Japanese words "te" (meaning hand) and "mari" (meaning ball), temari refers to the creation of beautifully embroidered thread balls. These exquisite creations were originally crafted as toys for children, but they have evolved into cherished decorative items and works of art.

In the world of temari, each ball tells a unique story, reflecting the skill and creativity of its maker. The art of making temari involves the meticulous wrapping of a core with layers of colorful thread, creating a solid foundation for the intricate embroidery that adorns its surface. These mesmerizing patterns range from simple geometric designs to intricate floral motifs, capturing the imagination and delighting the eye.

In this guide, we will explore the enchanting world of temari and provide you with step-by-step instructions to create your very own masterpiece. Whether you are an experienced crafter or a beginner eager to delve into a new artistic pursuit, making temari offers a rewarding and meditative experience that combines skill, precision, and creativity.

We will begin by gathering the essential materials needed to embark on this captivating journey. From the core of the ball to the colorful threads and embroidery tools, we will discuss each element required to create your own temari. Additionally, we will provide guidance on selecting the appropriate materials, including the ideal thread thickness, core size, and needle choices, to ensure the best results.

Once you have gathered your materials, we will guide you through the process of creating the foundational layers of the temari ball. We will explore the various wrapping techniques and share tips to achieve a smooth and even surface, ensuring a sturdy base for your embroidery. With a solid foundation in place, we will then delve into the art of temari embroidery, introducing you to different stitch patterns and techniques that will bring your temari to life.

Throughout this guide, we will share insights and tips from seasoned temari artists, providing valuable advice and inspiration to help you develop your own unique style. We encourage you to experiment with colors, patterns, and designs, allowing your creativity to flourish as you become immersed in this enchanting craft.

Whether you aspire to create temari as thoughtful gifts, striking decorations, or simply as a personal artistic pursuit, this guide will equip you with the knowledge and techniques to embark on your own temari-making journey. So, gather your materials, unleash your creativity, and prepare to be captivated by the timeless art of temari.

 Temari are embroidered thread balls that originated in Japan centuries ago. They are less tough to stitch than they appear - there are multiple steps, but none are particularly complex. Because there is no actual measuring involved in manufacturing Temari, there is no math! Temari can be any size, with an infinite number of pattern and color variations. Some patterns are considered to be traditional. We'll be making a traditional Kiku pattern, often known as a Chrysanthemum.

To construct a Temari, the ball is formed by winding yarn around some squishy substance. The ball is then separated and marked with thread and pins to prepare for the embroidery. The Temari design is then embroidered onto the ball.

Let's gather our supplies and construct a Temari!

Step 1: Gathering Materials

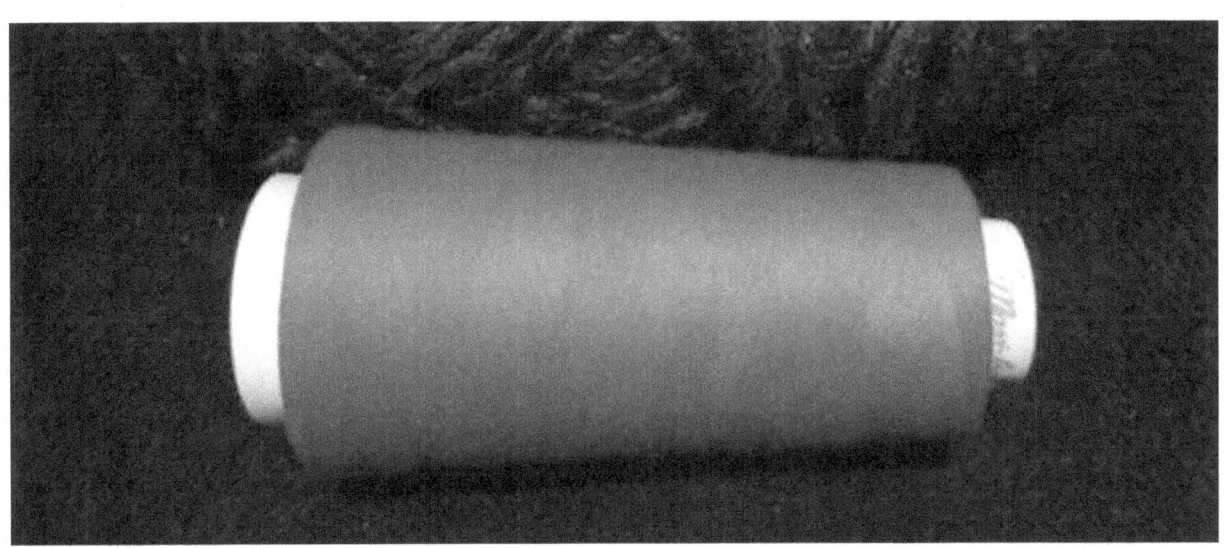

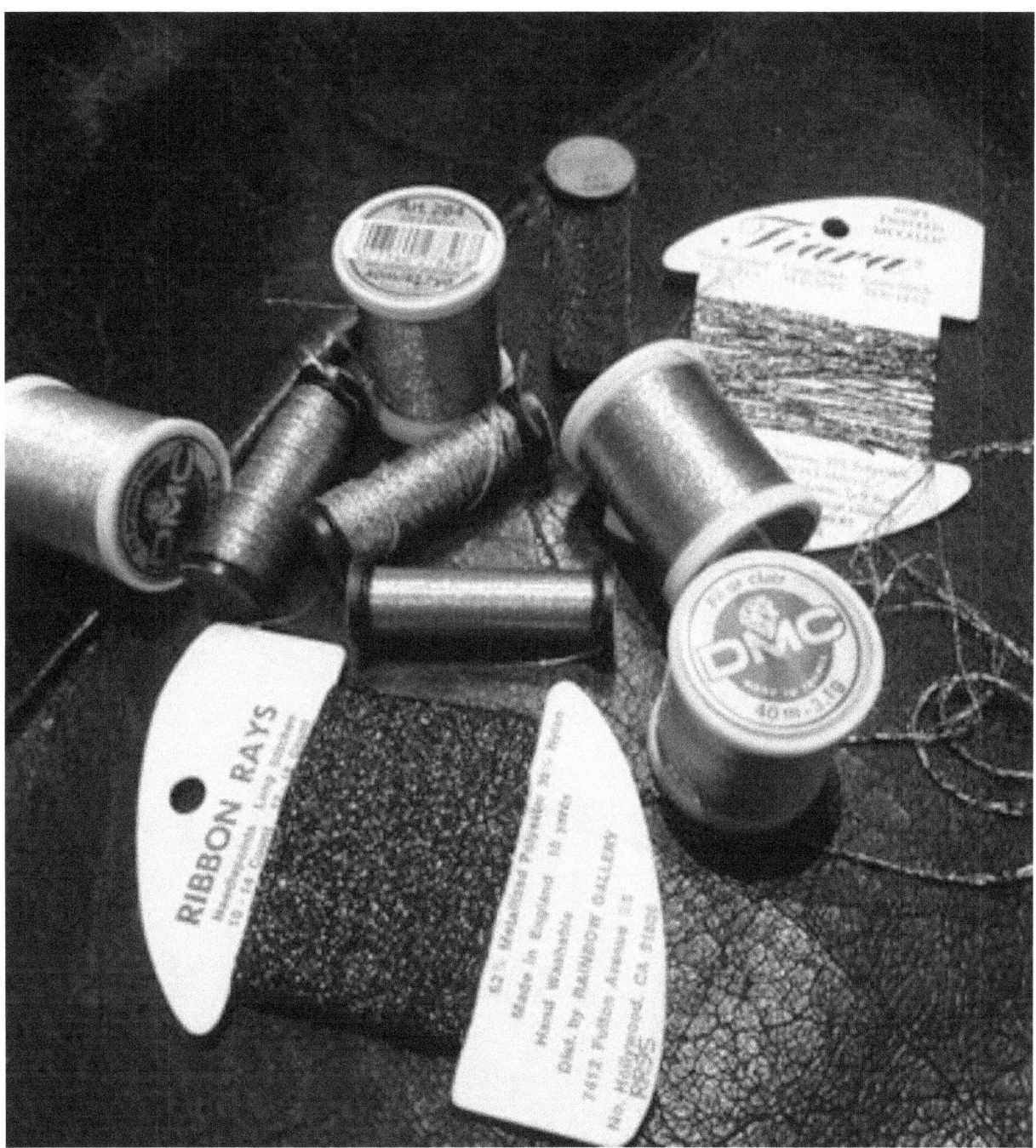

Temari's materials are simply limited by your imagination. Squishy materials for the inside of the ball, yarn and thread for wrapping (I prefer to have a color contrast between my yarn wrap and my thread wrap), and colorful/metallic threads for decorative stitching are all required. Threads and yarns can be found in craft stores, yarn shops, and needlepoint shops, as well as online. This is what we'll be using for Temari.

Primary Materials

- Fabric and/or yarn scraps - here is a fantastic spot to put all of those little cuts that seem to gather

Wrapping Supplies

- Yarn - nothing fancy because it won't be seen. Worsted weight or less
- Thread - sewing/serger thread - whichever color you want your finished Temari to be

Stitching Supplies

- One or more colors of perl cotton (sizes 5 and 8 work well). Available in commercial skeins/balls and from some fantastic indie dyers
- Metallic threads/braids that might be thin or thick

Notes: Dryer lint works well for the ball's base as well. Don't use your fine alpaca yarn for the yarn because it won't show in the completed Temari. You can use your odd bits and bobs of yarn, or perhaps that skein you've become tired of. Cotton, polyester, or a combination might be used for the wrapping thread. Serger cones of thread are useful since there is a lot of thread on the cone. For a baseball-sized Temari, I need a complete spool of 300-500yd (275-460 m).

Step 2: Resources

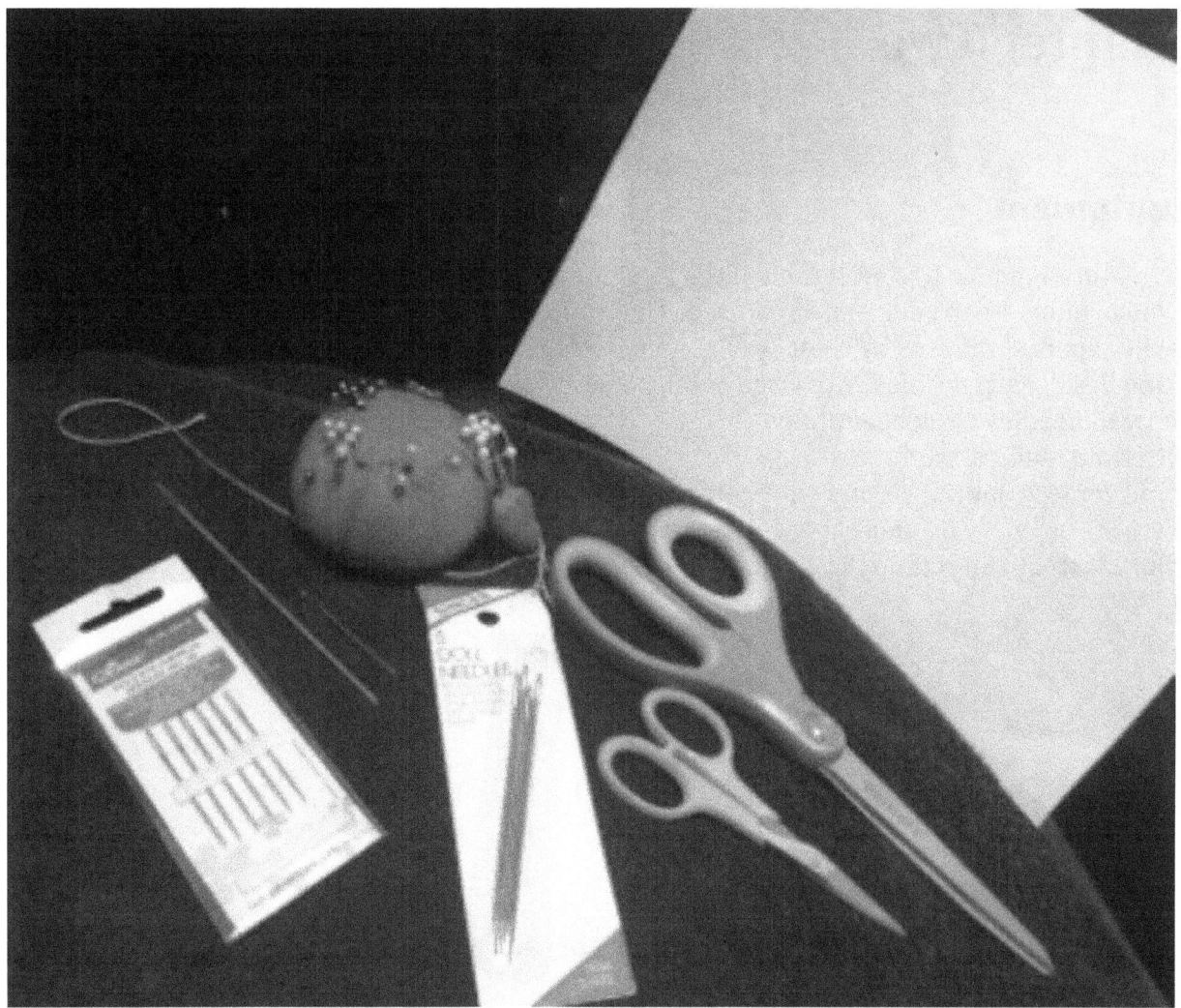

The tools required to manufacture Temari are relatively simple. You'll note there's no measuring tape since we'll "measure" our Temari with a simple paper strip (no math!). Here's what we'll require.

Chapter Two

Equipment

- A plethora of pins It is preferable if the pins come in a variety of colors.
- Pincushion - Keep your pins organized. The traditional tomato pincushion allows you to easily separate the pins by color.
- Needles - sharp needles with large enough eyes to hold your ornamental threads. Chenille and doll needles work beautifully.
- Scissors made of paper
- Embroidery/fabric scissors – for cutting decorative threads
- Paper - ordinary printer paper is adequate. I usually use white paper so that no dye from colored paper rubs off on the Temari.

Step 3: Make the Ball by Winding Yarn and Thread

It's a peaceful process to shape the ball that serves as the Temari's basis. Yarn and then thread are wound (and wound) around a squishy base to produce a sphere. When winding, it is critical to rotate and turn the ball continuously so that the yarn/thread is distributed randomly around the surface. This ensures that we receive a nice round ball. It will also provide as a strong foundation for our decorative stitching. Let's start winding!

Making the Ball Wrap in yarn

• Take a huge handful of your base material (I'm using fabric/yarn scraps).
• Wrap the yarn around the foundation material and start winding. Make sure to turn the lumpy ball with each wind of yarn.

- Wrap/turn, wrap/turn, wrap/turn. The lumpy ball will eventually flatten out into a smooth-ish sphere. Wrap/turn until the base material is no longer visible.

Thread it around

- Begin wrapping the yarn ball in thread. Continue wrapping/turning, wrapping/turning. I've discovered that putting the spool of yarn in a container keeps it from skittering all over the place.
- The thread will gradually cover the entire length of yarn. Keep wrapping/turning, wrapping/turning, and wrapping/turning until you think you're done.
- When you've used up all of the yarn, the ball should feel pleasant and smooth, and it should be quite round. The thread layers will accumulate and provide a beautiful stable layer for stitching.

Chapter Three

Secure the thread tail

• Thread the thread tail through a needle and anchor it by doing a few little back-stitches and burying your thread into the ball. Snip the thread near the ball.

Remember to have fun with your thread wrapping. Temari looks great in bright colors, or try blending threads. In the previous photo, the front left Temari base was wrapped with red and white threads.

Step 4: Cut the ball into sections and insert pins using a paper strip.

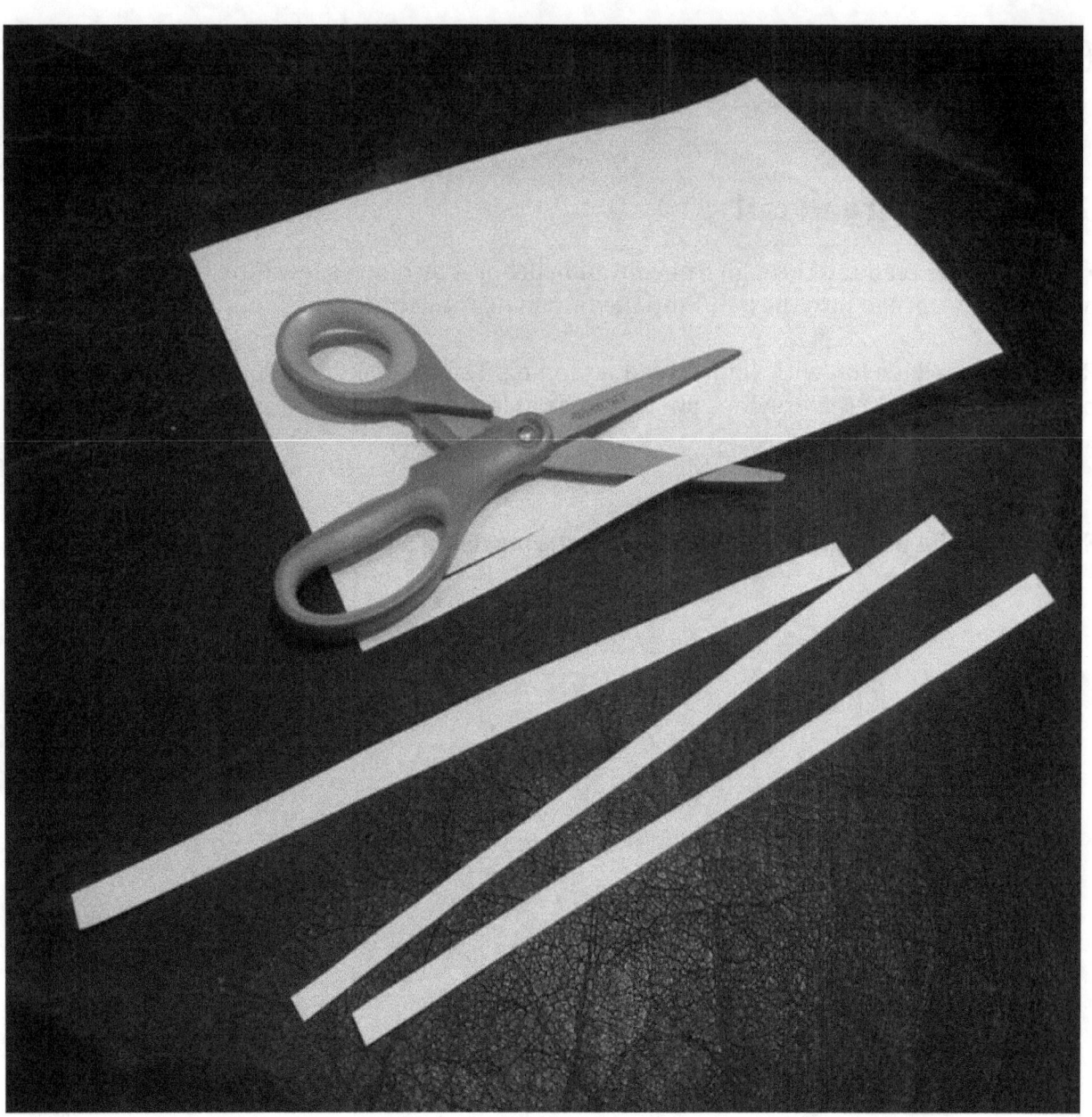

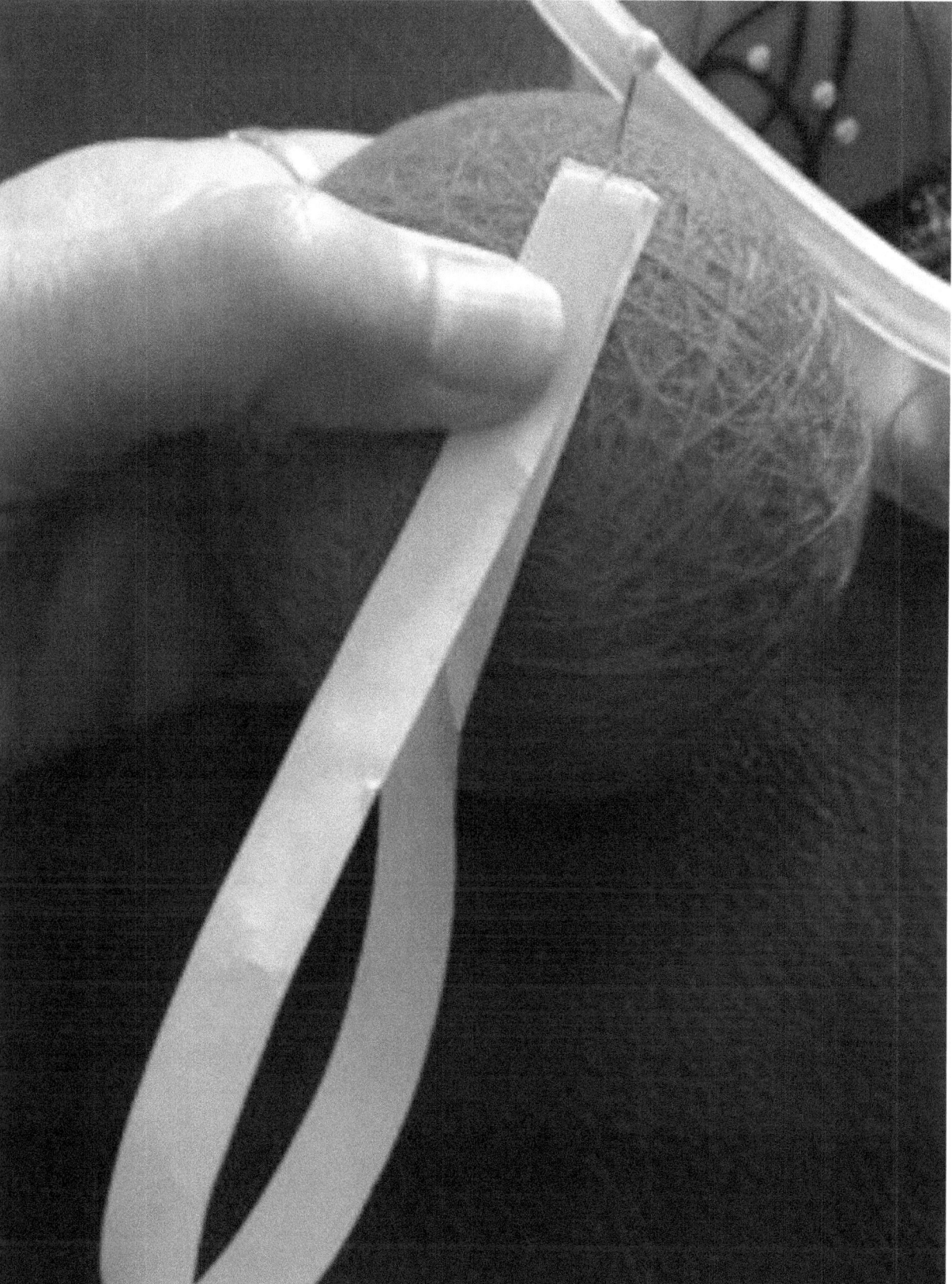

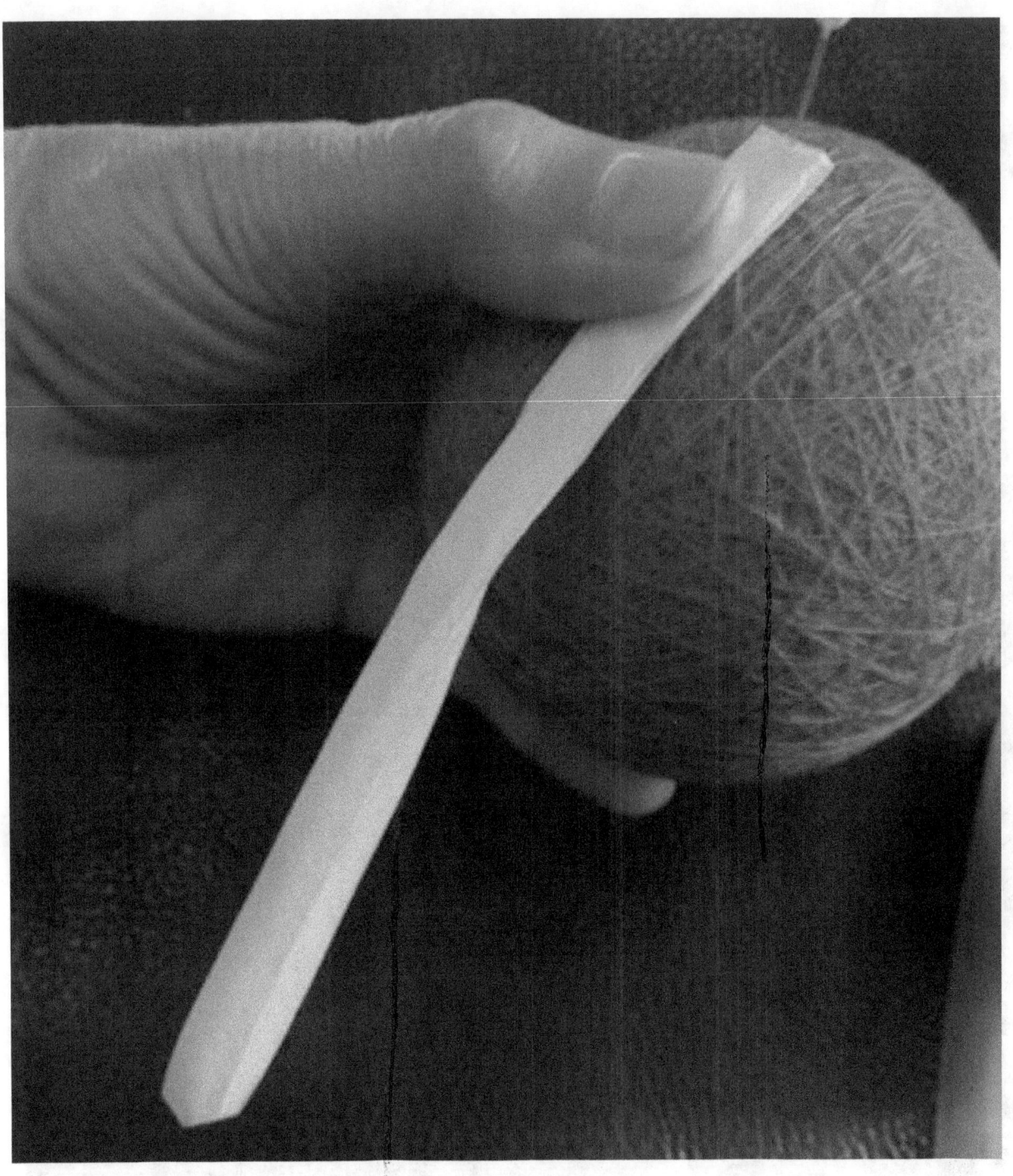

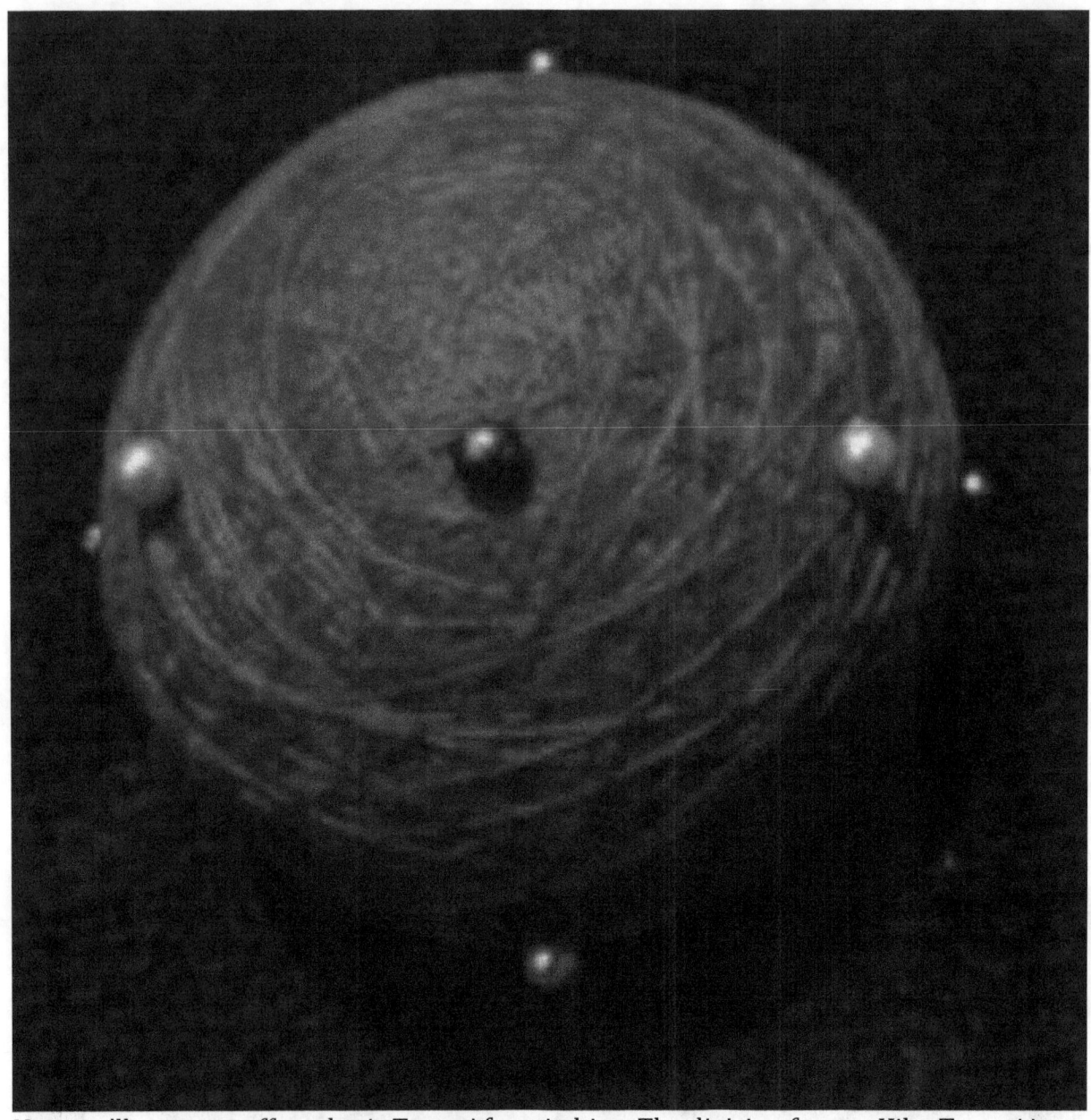

Now we'll separate off our basic Temari for stitching. The division for our Kiku Temari is known as a Simple 16; imagine dividing the ball into 16 evenly spaced orange segments. To make the divides, we'll use a paper strip. It also helps to conceive of the ball as a globe; we'll be describing our pin placements and defining the Longitude lines using the North Pole, South Pole, and Equator.

Make the paper strip for marking the poles.

• Cut strips 1/4" (6-7cm) wide, not completely straight; your strip must be long enough to go all the way around the ball; tape strips together for extra length if required.

Make a note of the Poles.

- Pin the end of the paper strip anyplace on the ball (we'll call this the North Pole).
- Wrap the paper strip around the ball and fold it against the first pin, then trim the strip.
- Fold the paper strip in half by pressing the end of the strip against the North Pole pin, then snip a notch into the strip at the fold to mark the halfway point.
- Wrap the strip around the ball again, and set a pin at the notch to mark the South Pole.
- Re-wrap the strip at another position on the ball to double-check South Pole pin placement - you may need to do this a few times to obtain a solid South Pole pin placement.

Chapter Four

Prepare the Paper Strip for Division Marking (orange Segments).

- Fold the strip in half again and snip another notch to indicate the fourths.
- fold in half and snip twice more to indicate the 8th and 16ths as well.

Make a note of the divisions (orange segments).

The first stage in dividing the land is to set pins around the Equator.
- Using your paper strip as a guide, slot in a pin at the Equator with the halfway notch positioned at the South Pole pin this corresponds to the ¼ notch on the paper strip.
- Rotate the strip around the North Pole pin and set another pin at the Equator; repeat until there are 16 pins around the Equator; don't worry if they aren't equally spaced yet.

We'll now use the paper strip to clean up the equator pins.

- Remove the paper strip from the North Pole and insert a temporary pin to mark the location.
- Wrap the paper strip around the Equator, then use the 16th notches to assist space the 16 pins evenly.
- Re-pin the paper strip to the North Pole and verify each pin to double-confirm the Equator placement.
- You may need to repeat these tests a few times before you're happy that the markings are evenly spaced - don't worry, this is normal.

You may also do a Simple-8 division (eight orange segments) instead. The last two photographs demonstrate pin placement for a Simple-8 division (red ball) against a Simple-16 division (grey ball).

Step 5: Cut the ball into sections and mark them with thread.

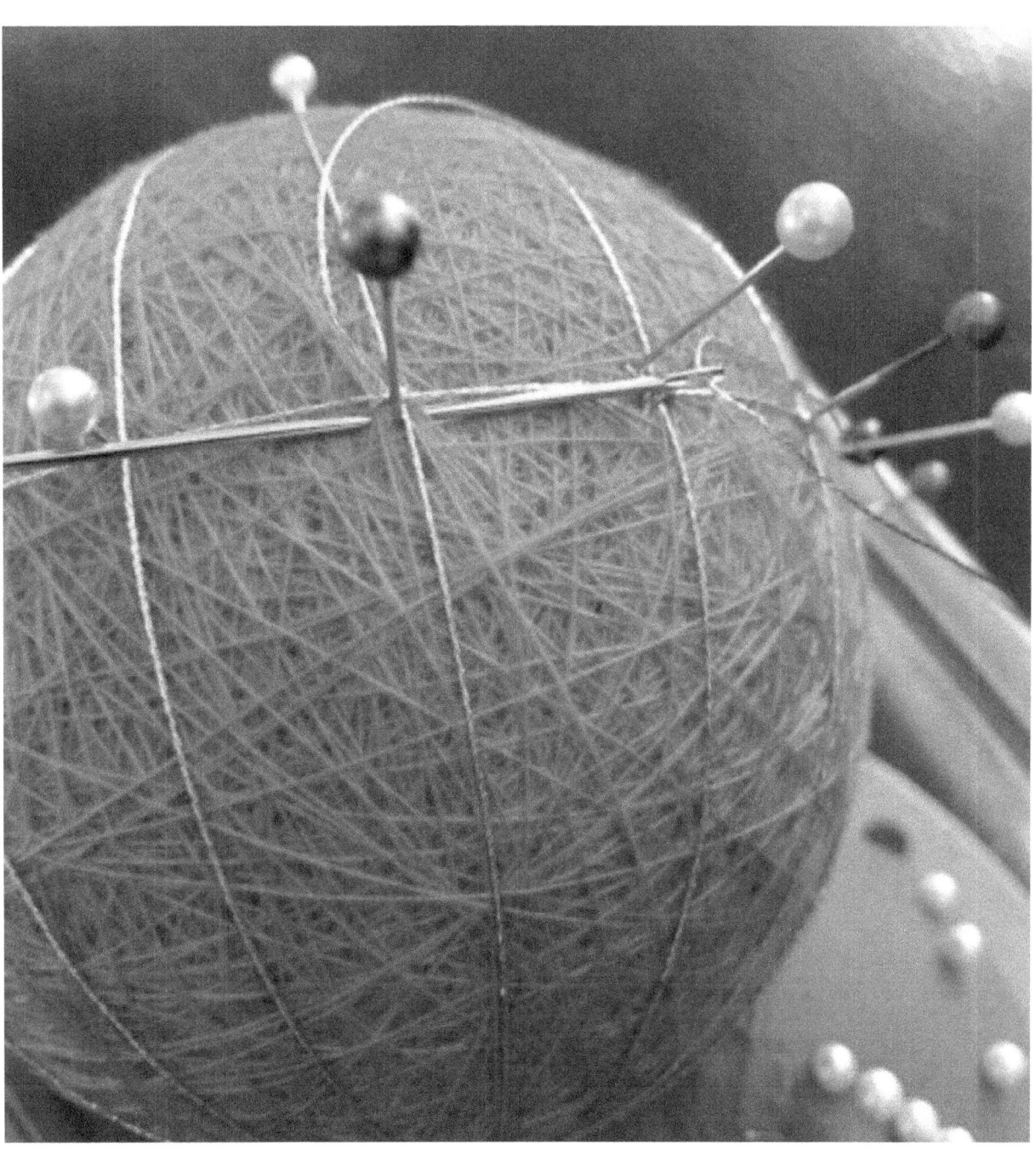

Now we'll use the pins as guides to draw some dividing lines on the ball. A thin metallic thread works well for this and adds to the ornamental aspect on the final Temari. We'll draw the lines first, and then secure them with stitches.

Chapter Five

Creating Divisions

- Wind your marking thread slackly around the ball nine times and then cut from the spool make sure that the thread length is very long to mark the divisions **orange segments**.
- Thread the marking thread through a needle and tie a tiny knot in the tail end
- anchor the thread into the ball by entering the needle into the ball a few inches away from the North Pole and bringing the point of the needle up as close to the North Pole as possible. pull the knot gently in other to hide it into the ball.
- Wind the thread carefully from the North Pole, through one of the Equator pins, past the South Pole pin, past the Equator pin opposite the first one, and back up to the North Pole, using the pins as a guide.
- Wrap the thread around the ball again, next to the Equator pins next to the previous wrap, and continue wrapping and pivoting around the North Pole pin until the ball is divided into sixteen orange segments **Longitude lines**.
- Anchor the tail of the marking thread into the ball by stabbing it into the ball and coming up a couple inches (5cm) away, then back into the exit hole and off in a new direction, snipping the tail of the thread close to the ball after a few direction changes.

Identifying the Equator

- cut another length of marking thread long enough to wrap three times around the ball, then unwind from the ball
- Thread this thread through a needle and tie a tiny knot in the tail end
- Anchor the thread into the ball by placing the needle into the ball a few inches away from the Equator pins and bringing the needle's point up as close to the Equator pins as possible. To hide and anchor the ball tug it into the ball gently.
- Using the Equator pins as a guide, weave the thread gently around the equator.
- When you return to the first pin, sew two little back stitches making a "x" across the Equator and Longitude lines to secure the Equator to the Longitude line.
- place the needle at the next Equator pin by passing it under the surface of the ball, hiding the marking thread behind the surface thread, and tack that spot with two little back stitches producing a "x" around the Equator and Longitude lines.
- Continue around the ball, tacking down at each Equator pin

Tackling the Poles

- Thread another length of marking thread through the needle - 18" (45cm) should plenty. At the end of the knot make a tiny thread.
- Continue to anchor the thread and get the needle up extremely close to the North Pole.

- Tack down the North Pole by doing little back-stitches in between the Longitude lines at the North Pole. Back-stitches should be placed between each Longitude line to secure the Pole. This will create a decorative thread bump at the Pole. As before, secure the tail end of the thread by making many direction-changing long stitches under the surface of the ball.
- Repeat same procedure on the South Pole.

Chapter Six

Mark Stitching Points with Pins

We'll now use pins to mark where we'll stitch. Each guideline will have a top and bottom pin for our Kiku Temari.

- Using the same paper strip, arrange it along a guideline and insert a pin into the first and second notch from Pole.
- Move the strip to the next guideline and insert pins into the first and second notch from pin 1.
- Continue until all guidelines have top and bottom pins.

Step 7: The Herringbone Stitch - Our Foundation Stitch

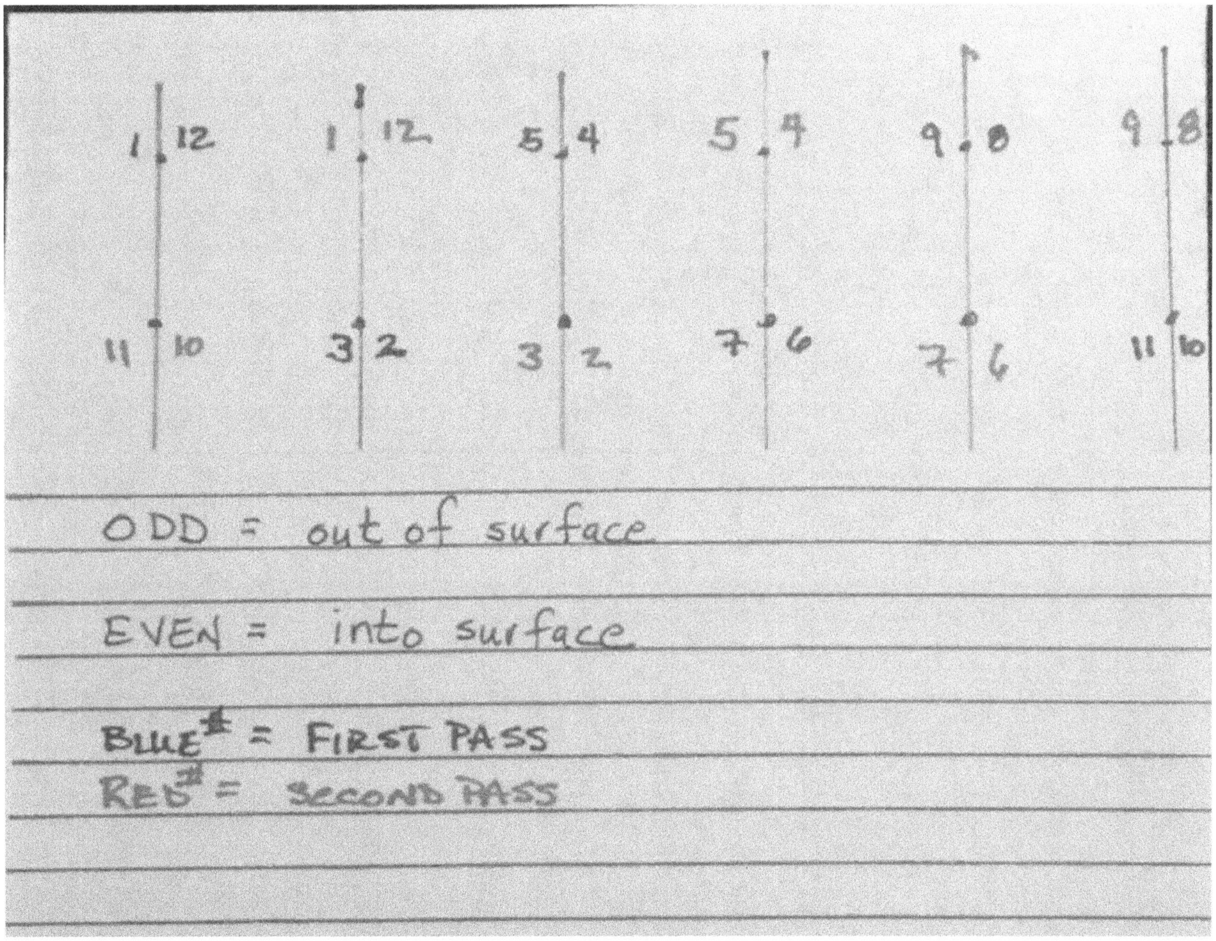

1 12
1 12
5 4
5 4
9 8
9 8
11 10
3 2
3 2
7 6
7 6
11 10
ODD = out of surface
EVEN = into surface
BLUE = FIRST PASS
RED = SECOND PASS

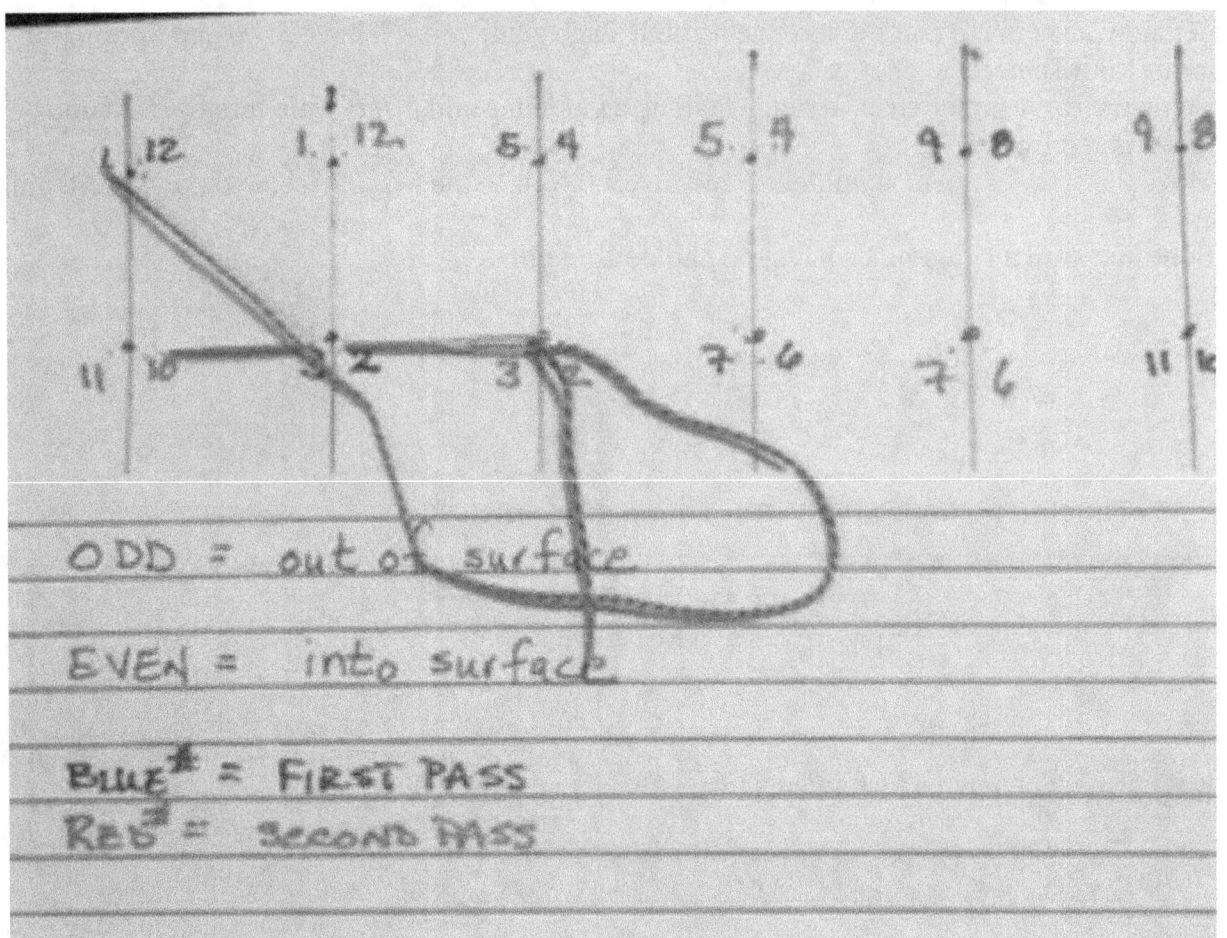

ODD = out of surface

EVEN = into surface

BLUE# = FIRST PASS
RED# = SECOND PASS

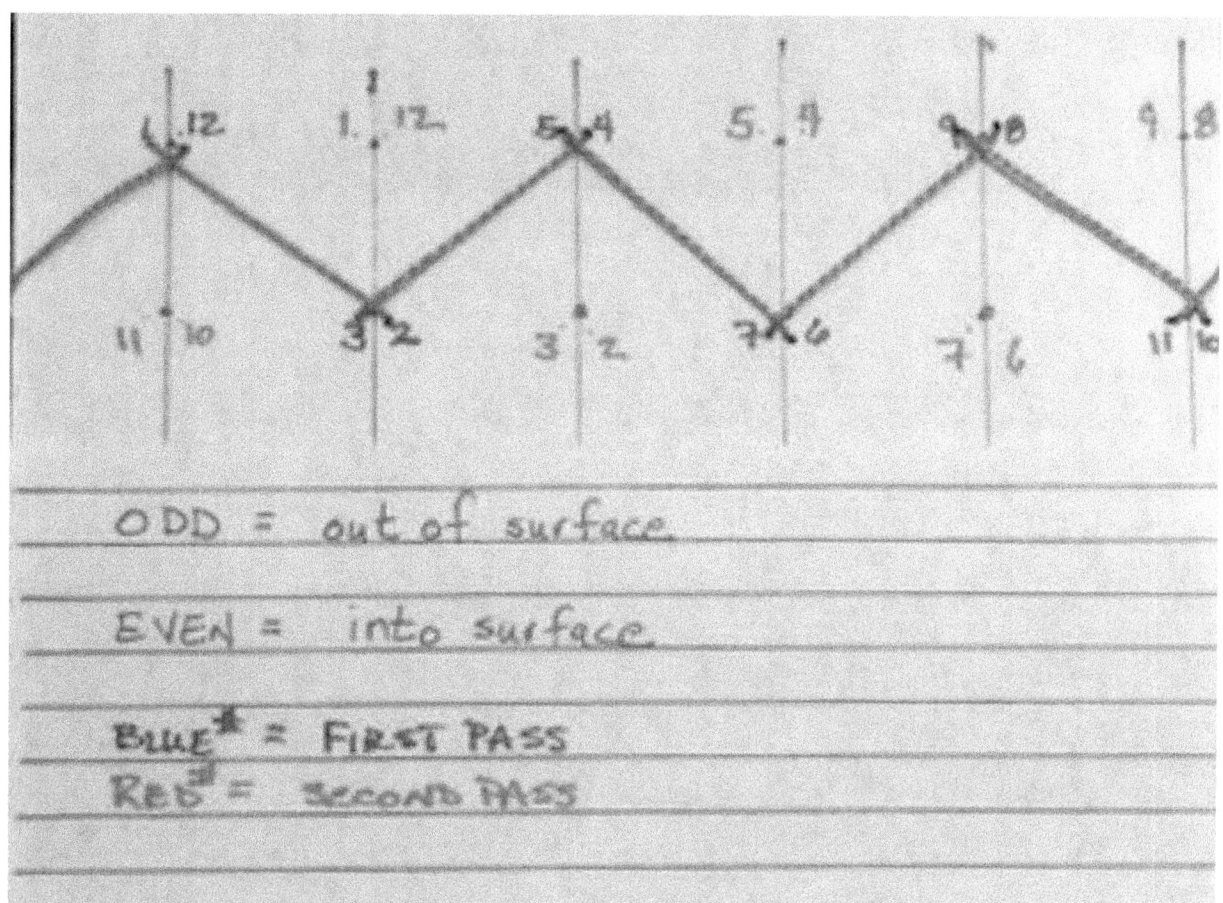

ODD = out of surface

EVEN = into surface

BLUE* = FIRST PASS
RED* = SECOND PASS

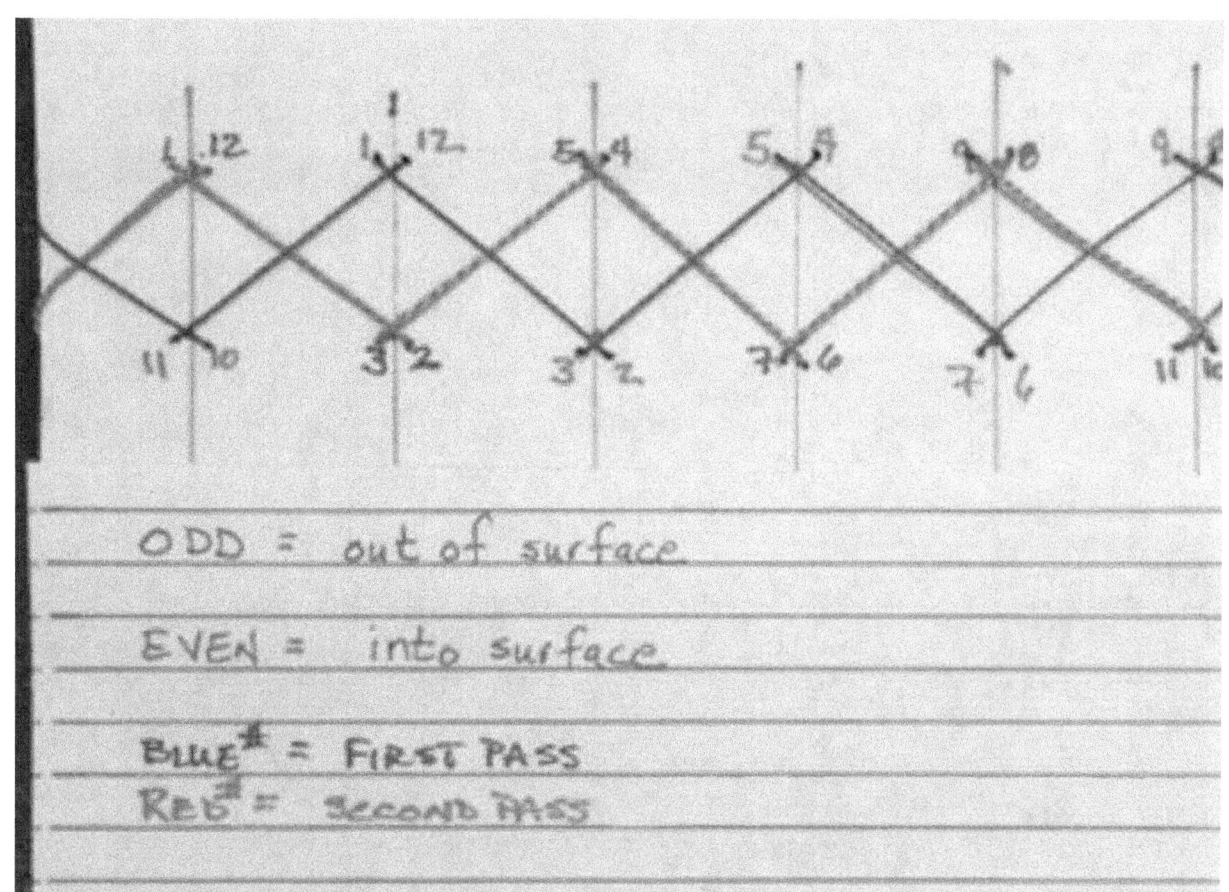

ODD = out of surface

EVEN = into surface

BLUE # = FIRST PASS
RED # = SECOND PASS

We'll be using a Herringbone stitch to produce this Temari ball. It's a simple stitch to produce; the photographs show a flat version on paper as well as how it will appear on the ball; we'll use this stitch to make the Kiku on our Temari.

Right-handers: Stitches will be taken from right to left, with travel to the right around the ball.

- tie a knot in the thread and bring it up to the left of the first guideline.
- slide the thread to the right and down - use your thumb to keep the thread where you want it.
- Make a small stitch from right to left around the guideline, keeping the needle perpendicular to the guideline.
- slide the thread to the right and up - use your thumb to keep the thread where you want it.
- Make a small stitch from right to left around the guideline, keeping the needle perpendicular to the guideline.
- slide thread to the right and down - use your thumb to keep the thread where you want it.
- Make a small stitch from right to left around the guideline, keeping the needle perpendicular to the guideline.
- You'll ultimately get back to where you started, completing the first pass. A continuous zig-zag line will be drawn around the ball (third and fourth photographs). End the round by inserting the needle into the ball; at this point, you can either finish or move on to the next set of stitches.
- To complete the first round, repeat the zigzag herringbone stitching on the alternate guidelines (second pass) so that each guideline has a top and bottom stitch (pictures 5 and 6).

We'll repeat these procedures for stitching on our Temari to add layers of colorful zigzags around the ball. These pointers will assist you with stitch placement:

- The stitches on each subsequent round are put BELOW the previous stitch at both the top and bottom pins.
- Place the threads with some space below the previous stitch at the bottom pins and use your thumb to hold the thread in place (seventh photo) - the natural tension of the stitches will cinch it up.
- Each subsequent stitch at the top pins is broader than the last. Look at the picture of the red and blue Kiku Temari; observe how the stitches at the top points flare out as they travel down.

Left-handers: Stitches will be taken from left to right, with travel to the left around the ball.

Step 8: Kiku Stitching - First Hemisphere

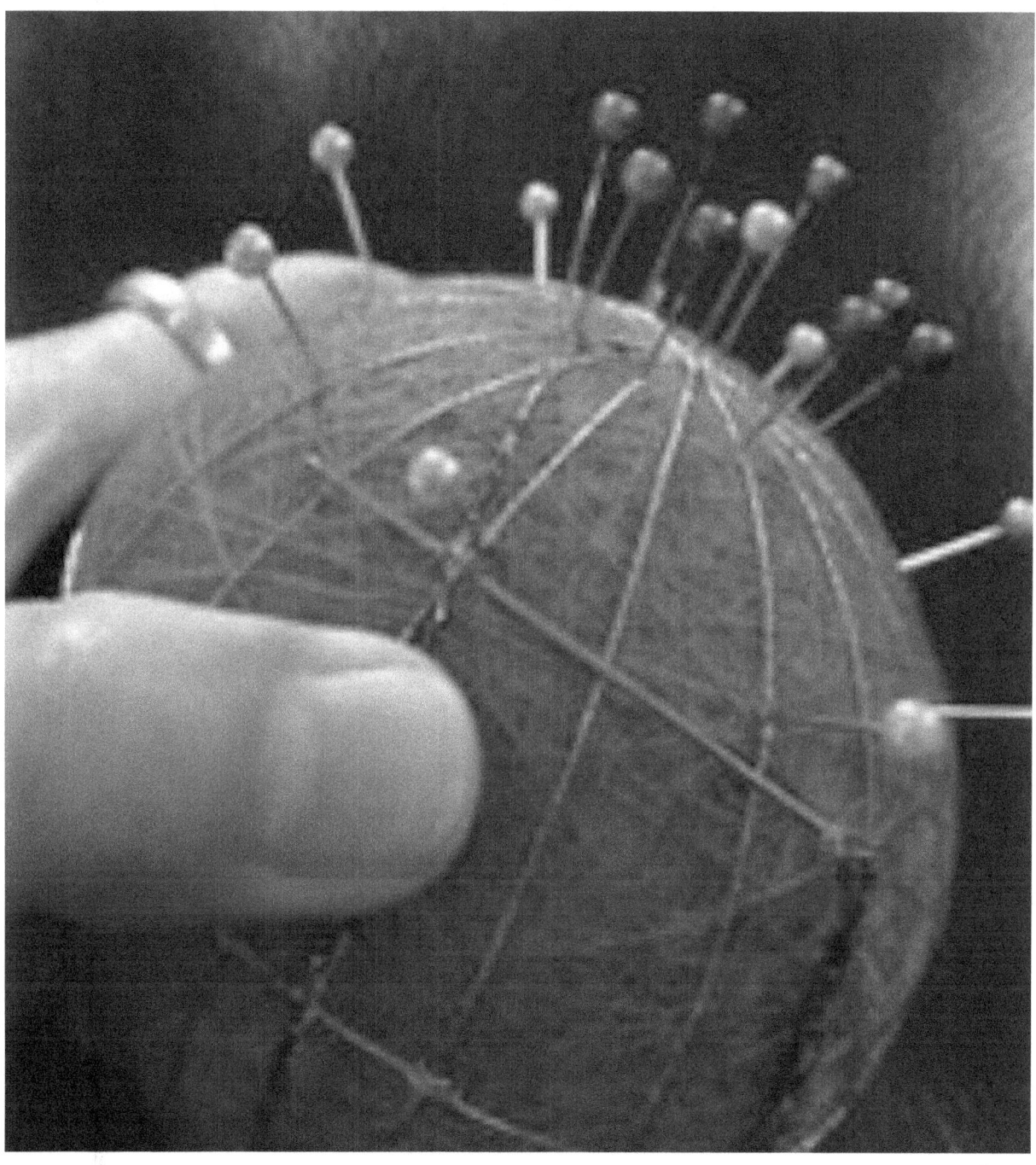

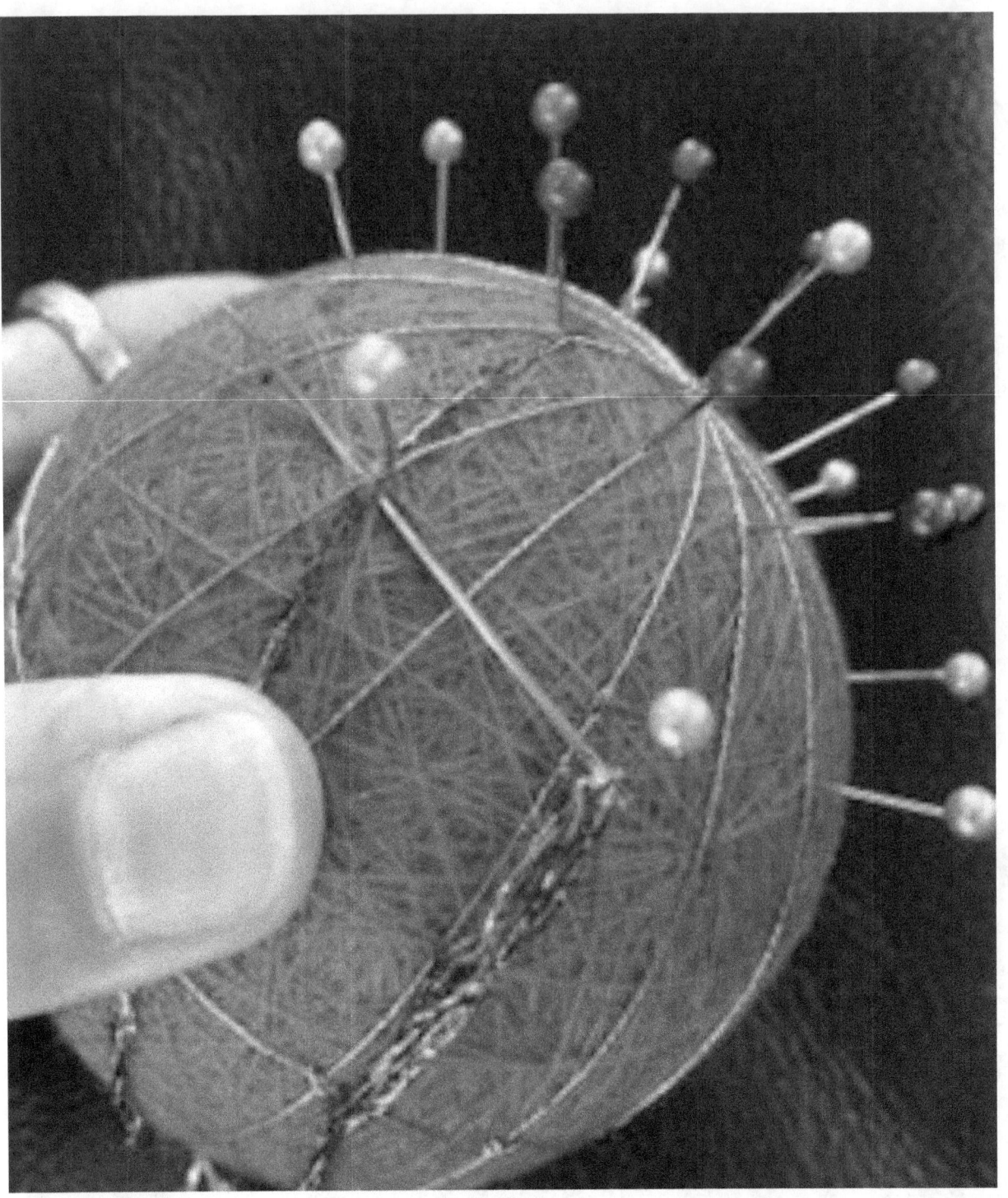

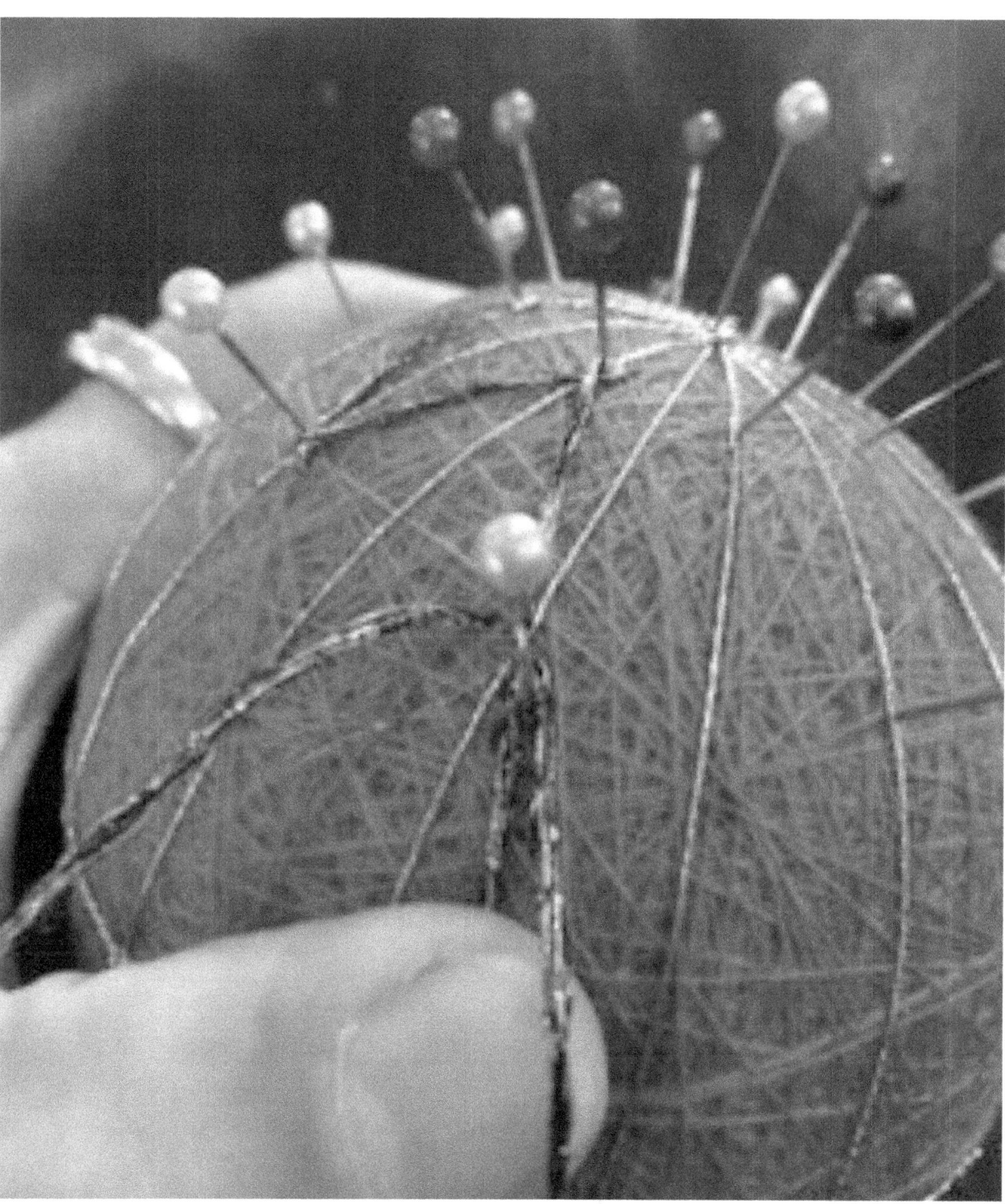

Now comes the exciting part: stitching our pattern, the Kiku! Use your imagination to choose your colors anything goes - I did six total rounds with two colors of perl cotton, thin metallic, and thick metallic. Don't be concerned if the pins grab your thread. This is typical. Simply stitch gently and remember to guide your thread with your thumb. Let's get started!

To make a Kiku, use the Herringbone stitch, changing colors as needed, then repeat the fundamental techniques for each circle. Each circle will require two passes to get top and bottom stitches around each guideline.

- **First pass:** from the top pin to the bottom pin stitch around the border line of the next Longitude line this will be the outcome in a continuous zigzag with top stitches on alternating guidelines.
- **Second pass:** sew around the guidelines once more, this time beginning from a top pin on a guideline that only had a bottom stitch from the first pass.

You should be able to remove the pins after two rounds. Without the pins, stitching will be much easier. The photographs depict the first several rounds as well as the completed Kiku.

Note: I'm going to repeat the previous step's advice because they truly are the key to stitching this design.

- The stitches on each subsequent round are put BELOW the previous stitch at both the top and bottom pins.
- Place the threads with some space below the previous stitch at the bottom pins and use your thumb to hold the thread in place - the natural tension of the stitches will cinch it up.
- At the top pins, each subsequent stitch is wider than the one before it, and the stitches flare out as the round progresses down.

Step 9: Kiku Stitching - Second Hemisphere

Our Temari ball already has a Kiku design around one pole, but we need to repeat it around the other pole.

Second Hemisphere Kiku Stitching

- As in the first hemisphere, place pins for stitch placement on each guideline.
- repeat the Kiku design - traditionally, the Kikus on each hemisphere match exactly.

Now that we've got gorgeous Kiku drawings on each hemisphere of our Temari, the area around the Equator is looking a little bland. We'll take care of it...

Step 10: Adding unique design Around the Equator and Decorative Stitches in Open Space

There are numerous ornaments that can be placed around a Temari's Equator. Obi are decorations that are placed here. We'll be using a basic wrapped Obi for this Temari, which will be held in place by a few widely spaced decorative Herringbone stitches.

Including an Obi

- Use ornamental thread to thread a needle. Tie a tiny knot at the tail end of the thread.
- Anchor the thread as before, and bring the needle tip up close to the Equator line.
- Wrap your thread near to the Equator marking thread around the Equator. Continue wrapping for as many rounds as you choose, setting each wrap directly next to the previous one and working your way outward from the Equator.
- Stabbing the needle into the ball and bringing the needle's point up close to the Equator on the opposite hemisphere will allow your thread to flow under to the other hemisphere.
- Wrap the Equator again on this Hemisphere.
- continue with additional threads as needed until the desired width of Obi is obtained

Protecting the unique design

- Thread another length of thread through a needle, tie a knot at the tail end, and anchor the thread as before, bringing the point of the needle up near to one edge of the unique design also known as obi thread and at a Longitude line.
- Make a little back-stitch around the Longitude line, then pull the thread over the Equator and make a small back-stitch two lines away at the Longitude line (this is a broad Herringbone stitch). Temari, repeat all the way around.
- Repeat these processes on opposing places until you have a series of **X** around the ball and over the Obi.

Using Decorative Stitches in an Open Area

- In the open space between Obi and Kiku, add ornamental stitches as desired. At each open spot, I've placed a few long back stitches.

Chapter Seven

completed Temari

The Temari is officially finished! In these photographs, I demonstrate a 16 point Kiku and an 8 point Kiku, as well as some of the other Temari that I've stitched. There is many different designs to find out! Both online and in print, there are fantastic resources for patterns, history, and how-to knowledge. The final image shows a few Temari books I've used, both in English and Japanese - there are many more authors. Even though I don't read Japanese, the Japanese books have excellent diagrams and can be followed once you've mastered the fundamentals of Temari.

Conclusion

In conclusion, temari is not just a craft; it is a testament to the rich cultural heritage of Japan and a celebration of human creativity. The art of making temari allows us to connect with the traditions of the past while expressing our own unique artistic vision in the present.
Throughout this guide, we have explored the fascinating world of temari, from its origins as a children's toy to its transformation into a cherished art form. We have learned about the essential materials and techniques required to create these exquisite thread balls, and we have discovered the joy of bringing them to life with intricate embroidery.
Making temari is a journey that invites us to slow down, focus our attention, and immerse ourselves in the process. It offers a moment of respite from the fast-paced modern world and allows us to find solace in the rhythmic movements of our hands and the vibrant colors of the threads. The creation of a temari is not only a labor of love but also a meditation, providing a sense of calm and fulfillment as we watch our creation take shape.
As you continue to explore the art of temari, remember to embrace your own creativity. Experiment with different color combinations, stitch patterns, and designs. Let each temari you create be a reflection of your unique artistic voice, telling your own story through thread and needle.
Whether you choose to make temari as a personal hobby, a means of relaxation, or a way to connect with others through thoughtful gifts, this traditional Japanese craft holds a special position in the hearts of those who practice the craft. It allows us to pay homage to centuries of tradition while leaving our own mark on this timeless art form.
So, let the thread guide your hands, and let your imagination soar as you embark on your temari-making journey. Discover the beauty that lies within the meticulously crafted thread balls, and experience the profound joy that comes from creating something truly remarkable with your own hands. Embrace the art of temari and let it weave its magic in your life.

www.ingramcontent.com/pod-product-compliance
Lightning Source LLC
Chambersburg PA
CBHW060427010526
44118CB00017B/2390